ANTHONY HOWELL · SELI

By Anthony Howell

POETRY

Inside the Castle 1969
Imruil 1970
Femina Deserta 1972
Oslo: a Tantric Ode 1975
Notions of a Mirror 1983
Why I May Never See the Walls of China 1986
Howell's Law 1990
First Time in Japan 1995

FICTION

In the Company of Others 1986

PROSE

Analysis of Performance Art 1999

AS EDITOR

Near Calvary: The Selected Poems of Nicholas Lafitte 1992

ANTHONY HOWELL

Selected Poems

ANVIL PRESS POETRY

Published in 2000
by Anvil Press Poetry Ltd
Neptune House 70 Royal Hill London SE10 8RF

ISBN 0 85646 324 8

This book is published
with financial assistance from
The Arts Council of England

A catalogue record for this book
is available from the British Library

Designed and set in Monotype Bulmer by Anvil
Printed at Alden Press Limited
Oxford and Northampton

Contents

ACKNOWLEDGEMENTS

'Sergei de Diaghileff' was first published by Turret Books, and it was later anthologised in *The Methuen Book of Theatre Verse*. 'Ticklishness' and 'Examining Mine, Imagining Yours' first appeared in *The Scotsman*; 'Animal Lover' came out in *Quarry* (Canada) as well as in *Antaeus* (USA), and 'Notions of a Mirror' was included in the PEN Anthology 1971–72. 'Femina Deserta' came out as a Softly Loudly pamphlet in 1971. 'Dreamt Lives' first appeared in *Vanessa* magazine, 'Privity' appeared in *Country Life*. 'Out Together' appeared first in *PN Review*. 'Nudes', 'The Age of the Street' and 'Out Together' were included in PEN *New Poetry 1* (1986). 'The Lost Garden' came out in *The New Statesman*. 'Nudes' also appeared in the Anvil anthology, *The Spaces of Hope*. 'Boxing the Cleveland' was first published by *The New Welsh Review*. 'The Ballad of the Sands' first appeared in *The Swansea Review*. 'Splices' came out in *Ambit*, and 'A Young Mother' was first published by *The Critical Quarterly* and was also anthologised in *The Exact Change Yearbook* (USA).

All of the poems included here have also already been published in books or in pamphlets, although I have only chosen to include one – 'Sergei de Diaghileff' – from *Inside the Castle* (Barrie & Rockliffe, 1969). The other early poems in this selection were included in *Imruil: A Naturalised Version of his Ode-Book* (Barrie & Jenkins, 1970), or in *Notions of a Mirror* (Anvil, 1983), while the later ones appeared in *Winter's not Gone* (The Many Press, 1984), in *Why I May Never See the Walls of China* (Anvil, 1986), in *Howell's Law* (Anvil, 1990) and in *First Time in Japan* (Anvil, 1995). Thanks are due to all the editors who have supported my work.

1

Sergei de Diaghileff (1929)

Sergei de Diaghileff (1929)

'Seroja, you're hurting. Hurt me!' Ach – I worried his arm
Against the dull class; trapped, worming, a
Wrist beneath lid. Provincial towns – Perm,
The desk-lid: grained geology of an Ernst or Dubuffet,
Neither of whom I admire. And no metaphor
Making of it a made theme. Compass-bored, elaborate
With sly graffiti. Myself bored with compasses.
Litter classified, schooling: 'Those cusps, crimped
Leaves; crisp as yeasty outside the window
They curl skyward. Say it. Say it!' – I levered him –
'Mathematics *is* unrussian!' Chinchilla.
And that was the one and only time the brigadier
Thrashed me. (Seroja broke my arm sir, he said . . .
He said) One duel I championed nature: memento.
Now strut, cultivate the strand.

'Je suis le spectre . . .' Gautier now. But what gold
Paved Peter's town! I skated, plump and suave.
Composition does not become me, since Rimsky insists.
Why not compose my friends? Mutely, imported aquarelles
Ignite the Stieglitz. That was before I invented
The avant-garde. 'Mir Isskoustva' . . . or some such aesthetic
Lab. Test-tubes to bung up Fokine, Benois
(Poor souls). I drew on my pipette and played them:
Compounded one with another to produce
That nonsense 'Armide': (effoliate the pavilion,
Tree-trunks as Louis XIV chair legs). Consider me
Neither as amateur nor dilettante. Am
The catalyst. Vatza decidedly
Lost his pants. The czarina ruffled (that was that).

The rose disrobes. I stripped the epiderm.
Never left nature her own devices (uncunning
Streams, leaves, have none). But folklorique as always
Our Russian brigades stormed the pelted,
Pelting tiers – where Astruc alternates blond with brunette.
The Châtelet repainted. No time to notice
Parisian May, I lounged in the stalls exhaustless.
'Je suis le spectre . . .' If so, Théophile, I shall haunt
Those stalls. Always to peel, to redefine,
In the light of the latest prodigy, my malaise.
With less of an idea have now than had,
What constitutes. So many prodigies have modified
Since then. Where Cocteau rhymes to define
Nijinsky dances. Oh, the dread and horror of their task!
My own abilities hinder. All theirs is mine, my
Papillons, pastiches. Wand white I have abandoned.

Now wheel me out on the verandah. Those,
Incidentally charcoals, are by – but of course you know.
Breathing! How I care more now (late my day)
For air. But not too clear and rare and precious.
This hot-house of a lagoon suits me, with
Its air fin-de-siècle and unhealthy. '. . . de la rose
Que tu portais hier . . .' which I carried,
Have abandoned. Carry the spectre.
Reproach my self-indulgent tears, while what's
His wife's name? Romola? – stupid, stupid

As a woman, as the droves of swans, gulls, geese,
Heckled and departed in their own brief lights
To clack in frippery: fluttering companies
Which ignore the lighthouse! Pavlova. And that
White pear, that Rubenstein! With just as much mobility
As a pear, whereas to be danced
Around she made a fine shrine. Must have
Her way and rolls about the stage – to Stravinsky

(The one man Rimsky might allow compose,
And who repaid him kindly!) Poire en lieu de grenade
Was gingered. Sugary through and *all* through
That fool Leon! As Romola: 'Jew to be sure,
But he was also something of a genius.' (Bakst).
How should *she* know (of genius)? From the day
Her 'rose' proposed she was at sea. The ninny!

'. . . que tu portais hier . . . au bal.' Spectre,
This morning shall preamble. A blue God
Incenses me in the Lido . . . Make those French windows
Taller, take away the bird! The rose's elevation
Elevates. Should seem incongruous he remind me here,
A creature essentially Russian? Not so
Incongruous to be here perhaps? Hand me those delights
Which tease my doctors – follow my finger, over where
A boy rises on his toes – those insteps – as the foam
Covers them, at the Lido's margin; leotard
For swim-suit. A Picasso. (Do you know him? Has designed
Several.) See him for himself, unsigned. A body by Nijinsky.

'Vatza, mais tu es paresseux.' Purr, purr,
'Mais viens, viens. J'ai besoin de toi.' 'Je ne peux pas
Car je suis fou.' Listen to Sergio recite his visions
'Du Baller Russe'. Vatza, Vatza
Has taught me how body is sterner,
More morally severe than mind bewitched
By lascivious environs: mimosa
Shaking its plaits over the hill's shoulder, something
In the air; immediate realisation of breathing this or that
Crisp morning; pillars emerge from mist – how body
May refuse, say look, say listen to the first,
The first ray, bird wing skip the water, the first motes
Rising serenely on their long journey to the sun. That day
In obese mirrored, guilty apartment. Moscow:
My art-junk; too many ikons, long since abandoned,

Forgot. Me naked. Him naked
And his eyes. I would have pomaded, paraded before that mirror,
Instead, his body's remonstrance. I parodied.
For his oblique eyes drew lids, for once revealing
Stavemarks where a Slav tune trod adagio and lightly,
To which his fear was counterpoint;
A spoiling innovation, nervously nouveau. He had

A body on him which could utter – I'm losing words. Help
Me drink . . . better. Yes, could utter at its most inactive
(Seated, say shifting slightly the weight), or most riotous
'Igor', a complete silence as of the steppe
Pacing, pacing effortlessly towards invisible pole.
He spoke with such a lump in the mouth
There must have been God in him. And the God
Was body – but not a permissive, Bacchic –
A 'but', admitting of no excesses, sighing for all the world
His nailed limbs. A question, anxious for his starved
Beasts taken for glue in the factories
Whose smoke spirals, nooses the steppe in hemp.
(And the noose closed on the dancer.)

The mirror tarnished. Room shrank from his presently
Into frowsy antiques. Routed, the array of china,
Bell-tassels, gaslit candelabra . . . Diabetic now in Venice,
The white Russian with the lacquered hair
And a taste for . . . certain tastes is, am still, abashed.
The God, my Hellenic reason, stared me
Down. Failed my slipshod, already corpulent.
I, the eloquent, darling of every spa from Dieppe to 'Petrograd',
Say with my body, what? The neurotic flesh
Speechless than incoherent compared to his. A
Congenital vegetable! The intelligence,
Knowledge and memory in his flesh. It was Stravinsky.

Was the Urals, shawled, with no more fathers,
Husbands, sons, left to bury.
And the paradox: a Romany whore, swings bells,
Roubles, bosom, back to her surly. (Also the bull lines
Somewhere; the sad circus's attic animalry
Of that young Spaniard mentioned earlier. His
Primary blue, his Mediterranean 'as above Gourdon
That day.' His centaurs stamping
The beach). Was river, sky, pine-sweat,
But would not use these as a seasonal excuse
For poetry, the legs' laughter, clothes strewn
Over a rug . . . My cigar
Singed an overweight chair.

I dressed shabbily. Remember how his hand
Reached for, held, turned the door handle.
Then the door closed. The door
Has remained closed. It took some time to conquer
My body's shyness, his own temerity
In these matters. But the door refused, refuses
When tenement crumbles. Water!
He became confident, sly. We were several times,
How many hours, I can assure you, happy.
But I, my body, never learnt that language.
For with the first closing of a kiss something else
Should open. Darkness be broken into like a tomb.
I never hooked fingers, tugged and prised

My lazar house. Inarticulate half moan, the most
My preserved limbs managed – after intense effort –
Words as if for water, loudless, infirm, less
Free than my throat hobbles them now.
And that once I may imagine (only) remember
In Paris. Had no desire to dominate but to speak.

To speak, keep with me. (This afternoon
Rodin invites you as a faun to his conservatory).
To keep him, dominate, in some way: silence.

A death at sea? I venture to the shore,
No further; was a death certainly
Aboard ship – his departure.
How the meaningful sea has deceived me.
With Amérique du Sud, engagement, exile.
I puffed up silky: an extremely clumsy panther, dumb
with body, rage;
Having become powerful in his world.
Now R introduces him to acupuncturists
While I weep – petulantly.

More Nijinskys, noces; more strident origins, more
Prodigious Russians. All prodigal: bitches, cocktail hours,
Balanchines. I know few dancers (and I have known many
In several ways) who could approach his mother tongue,
Which nothing trains nor breeds. Have seldom spoke
So guileless when I say, Have seen
Such speech. Any may dance, but rhetorically. Who knows
If style is what matters, especially now,
Since I turned bookish, shelving . . . ?

Venice sets as the sun raises a haze.
Glimmer of hooves, St Mark's drawn into fog.
The day raises sandy and treacherous . . . . . . That boy,
Towelled after his morning, mounts the frail,
The soon to be footed shore. Here I am,
Spectator of my last cotillon; a
Portly butterfly, sedate above the spume. Frail wings
In the mist – a perfect Balanchine? – Merde!
Water me. Ramasse mes oreillers!

2

Ticklishness

The bird she cannot bear
Walks with tiny strides
Attacking here a grain.
Her belly shrinks before
Suggested promenades
Of its feathery idea.

But such a tease as this
No ocean dare resist
Or lunatic ignore.
Imagine either fate:
An overbalanced wave,
Asphyxiating mirth.

Surrender is a fort.
The cornered ball uncurls
Inviting beak to nest.
This confuses predator
With timid prey impaled
Upon a broken sword.

Animal Lover

1 *Without Titles*

[i]

Crepuscular.
Her rationale the non-competitive cheetah's.
(Intellect of absolutely no importance
Except as it affects certain external flexions.)

The mouth, shaping for its own benefit
A variety of syllables.

[ii]

Hot-blooded diet, parded love
That could never adapt to prosaic situations
(Pavements file down the claws)
Nor survive the tritest of breakfasts.

2 *Towards Night the Jungle Laps the Waterhole*

Aubades haunt the aviary.
Those who are accustomed to devouring darkness
Slide into each other for repose.

(The well fed, meticulous hubbub
Of the herd – snufflers at the trough
Indulge in trunky intercourse.)

Hatred in epitome, or is it love:
The way those big cats mock
The meat of their keeper?

3 *Six Legged Odalisque with Wings*

[i]

Freedom: a regressive sense
That manacles her to herself;
Haggard blood paces out a constitutional
Against the ribcage.

This is the innermost, arcane
Gymnopedia. Butterflies
In the tummy cause her to rest
A hand on the escorting wrist.

Touch and the wings fold.

[ii]

When the tigress dare not venture
Without a mask to lull censure,
When those insipids, the butterflies
Make up their much wider eyes,

Flirt we then in the moon's mirror,
The bed, the retentive pool,
The killing bottle: facets blur

All living stones, my pet, and clever
Boys with gauze to catch you in
Shall fix the pin;
Spread your wings to dry forever.

4 *The Decalogue Forbids Idolatry*

Nothing cleans the key to an inadmissible
Room, and it is only a fool
Such as Francis talks to animals;
Thus she preserves the vault's quiet

(Her breath waking no echo) as
The vault preserves us, all the more

Abandoned in her sleep – a beautiful gibbon.
Turned from the peaceable kingdom,
The wolf would have her stroke his whisker,
Howls for a glance, if not the look

That changed his mate to salt.
Let me insist, there are no true idols.

Notions of a Mirror

1

Yes, you can take that away,
But leave the similar objects as they are
– Visibly, they fill themselves.

It all exactly fits:
Here, and there
A mass of shapely things.

And those, in a trance of manifestation
Rocketing from their place,
What are they called?

2

Each deep face
Echoes our own feelings
– Rather than drink you in

An urge to whisper nothings:
"Call me a Wishful, nevertheless
We might be little

Better than relations,
Even the blinds display a space as querulous,
There is no room for more."

Examining Mine, Imagining Yours

Hand on the left will make no sign
Of movement unless sure
The route affords strategic pockets
Vital to retreat: it treads
With a sloth's anxiety,
Fixed in a bright globe of quiet.

Right hand relies on tactics:
Crouches to consider,
Jumps! Brutally severe, he curls
And spreads his nails, attesting claws
That basked within a carcass.
Wrist he may mistake for throat.

That hand's unblinking charmers,
Stroking the callous palm
Just as one should the belly of a cat;
This hand's jungle, vase of flowers,
Nesting the sloth in fingers
Curious as a team of naturalists;

Scornful of strait-jacket gloves;
Not animated puppets but
Supporters of unstable gods:
Firm as ancient clouds, your hands
Hover on their jointed stems
Like thoughts difficult to arrange.

Extraneous Fixtures

Tenements where everything is repaired
Except the tenants. What are they
But weights for the resident furniture
To be sat on by? Nor may they strain
The divan plump with maladies,
For what they wear they do not own.
Dish-washers hardly deal with dishes.

Each house helps another up the hill:
No tenant asks for like support
From neighbours when to slip outside
And rap the nearest door allows
Absence to enter theirs and change
The lock and key to all that's loaned –
More phantom then, being exorcised.

How flat the stare, daring no smash
Though trains trail goods in bulk across
Embankment windows and the sun
Sit in each park to keep it warm:
These tenants waste such hours indoors
Mere body heat they fade from chairs,
And poplars shake like displaced souls.

Femina Deserta

The Maker takes his one siesta
In this idle country bare
Of milk and honey, mud and straw:

A garden where the presence of
Proprietor diminishes
The space elsewhere embedding things.

Does meditation magnify
A moment or elaborate
Events to dress the poverty?

The mind's a spider in this heat:
Metaphor's geometry
Must extend a lengthy net,

Whose rigging may intend towards
A hillock where a certain bush
Is said to quench the thirst with fire –

But nomads in retirement stare
Beyond the littered littoral
Where shepherds reprimand their sheep:

They tell of cairns reviewing cairns
Already seen, and further still
A riddle waving eager tall:

Underneath whose haunches fur
Explains the smell that captivates
Aroma conscious bedouin:

Holding a breath for ever and ever,
Saturating lungs
Jealous of what each inhales.

Pernicious breeze in nostrils able
To divine a lost oasis
By the reek of its mirage.

Here Solitude herself remains
Inert – for all the splash of pails
In the well available.

Guess ahead, suppose a city
Helmeted with mosque,
Flinging the lance of its minaret.

But will a hand succeed in crossing
Such a virginal expanse
While struggling against repose?

Perhaps the never pictured mosque
Which rinses clean all vision stained
By naked light cannot appear?

The further place forbids a visit:
Dwellers there may be supposed
To own no word for boundary;

Where afternoons direct migrations,
And each profile of tall bone
Gives away an obvious name,

And if and when a finger twitches
Surfaces of satin stir
In hieroglyphic labyrinths.

But as we near the stranger stars
Our singers cease to innovate:
They pause at more familiar nouns.

A savage blaze upon the forehead
Of a brigand's horse describes
That ambush which the sun prepares:

Before whose rampant haze the date road
Falters. Our approach explodes
The landmarks – into old dry birds.

The desert thinks the vultures limping
Over her reflection are
The pockmarks of her dry oases.

Horror in the gleam of joy
That blinds the fly who crawls among
Her lips towards a laser tongue!

At arm's length is the sun whose grin
Certifies he values her
Above his other predators.

She turns away, inviting night's
Brown eyelids down to soothe the shells
Azure as mosques, her nested eyes.

Hip to hip she lies with night
Though envious of the splendid gouts
Replenishing his open mouth;

Her own reserve is curdled somewhere
Silent – and for this her nerves
Must go to vague extremities.

That she may blossom at the tight
Antipodes of every root
Sky becomes a tree of rain:

A thunder tree that clenches cloud,
The torso of a liquid god
Which branches out in muscled flood,

And shakes the fledglings from her shells
Till tunes revolve like little pins
Arranged around a cylinder.

The desert stretches forth her neck
And shifts her weight – a sluggish ocean
Pleased the rudder alters her.

Then cacti germinate and fix
Their sets of brooches there before
The miracle evaporates

In sand whose tautly hollow sound
Is evidence, although an ear
Will never prove the reservoir.

Such secrecy envenoms flesh
And suckles what prefers to wriggle
Like a vein, immersed in dust.

No faithful dove invades these waves
To whisper the obscenities
Of any charming rainbow demon.

Flash! The thunder came and went.
That momentary deluge seemed
A phantom of annunciation.

Mockeries of vegetation
Are engendered thus, to jilt
Her thirstiness and leave her frozen.

Leave her freezing in the sun
Whose cymbals deafen when they clash,
While fever beats its rapid drum:

Fever which insists mosquitoes
Darn upon her famished realm
A needle-pointed zodiac:

Because without one stitch of green
Embroidery, spread-eagled, bound
By thongs which tighten while they dry.

A kind of shame, the drought chastises
Wilderness, that naked ground
Where revelations feel their way.

Loss of a Language

Before it shut, your mouth
Uttered the last word.
Darkness covered your face,
The distressed waters
Writhed like incensed adders.

Overstrung, the crack
Of each high tension wire
Blackened night:
Our bridges bucked,
Many a road ran wild.

How did who return?
Wading the knee-deep lakes
To touch familiar walls
Strange with green, while roads
Waited in immense reels.

Sewage foams at the tap.
Furniture and sheep
Glide beyond our reach
Beneath the empty bridges
Polished of graffiti.

Left with an aftertaste
Of unremembered names
Bitter as salt for sugar.
Dong, bong, dong.
The tongue lurches in a tower.

Dreamt Lives

And always saying no to say everything,
Never nodding to affirm, and to deny everything,
Forever not at home, not to say anything,
Hardly conversational, and to affirm anything
In narrow clean mansions forever not at home.

You decayed in an untidy house
Fattening on the highways among friends
Who grew up in rambling stables: and to affirm anything
A market place with unknown rooms,
Accessible departments and outdoors.

Who grew up admitting less?
– Refusing every bit in rambling stables,
And among hermits who died in private alcoves
Among lovers and deserted squares
With known rooms and never saying no.

I was to begin my life, you decayed
In constrained circumstances, nodding and outdoors:
Dwindling in alleys among enemies
Taciturn about the lot in small neat houses
– To say just that among the angels.

I flourished in a neat house,
Accepting all that came saying nothing,
Voluble about the lot, and affirming nothing,
And never saying no, silent about little,
Shaking head seldom and outdoors.

An untidy house among the angels
Who lived in large untidy houses,
You were to end your days in a wild expanse
Among brutes who died among friends
In a tame cage I was brought up in.

And admitting less, loud about all and
Shaking head forever, quiet about all,
Silent about little, to say just that,
Taciturn about the lot, and to affirm the lot,
In constrained circumstances I was to begin my life.

You succumbed in a dirty hut
Saying nothing among brutes who died
Accepting all that came in small neat houses
– And never a garden, secreting hidden cells
Or public precinct vast with open air.

There You Are

So if you must be you you must
If you're the way you're feeling
Not that you can say for sure you never
Met this you of yours the loneliness
Of you all and what have you
Cutting you loose from all yours
Except yourself of course
You the paths you can't imagine
Mellow delight of you discovering
What you meant when you sat with this back
To that your look equivocating
About whose front yours was
Well you might while you were slowly

What are you on about now why ask
The usual how do you do how are you
Ever to say you never can tell
With the likes of you who never saw
Your like yourself you with your face
Like an amphitheatre quite beside yourself
Wherever you sat you might remind
Your you know what that here you went back
On yourself to your earlier you
You and your recital yours throughout
You see your abrupt your mock violence
Like talking through a brick wall

An Angry Blue

How to be reason, how to be hopeless in light:
Exhaustion throwing off the bad
Other proposals – letter to get off
To people of pedestrian letters, petitions

Somebody causes out of gas bills, *idées fixes*.
Falling and tardiness in keeping up
Dental floss, feet. Highly strung times
To sit still through for long enough, guilt about

Times unstrung when one can't get up
In the shambles that has somehow ended up.
Of a kitchen of the body – blisters, bruises,
Spots brought on by not changing to be

Bright for all efforts to prove oneself
A citizen . . . that has been denied fellow citizens.
Without blame. Imagination, a dirty enough
Word, an education, it elbows. And walls

Of the innumerable discomforts brought about.
But sleepiness, the fading eyes, the heavy.
Heavy to waste an hour, the mending
Of petty ruptures, all the tasks –

How to be hated, having no whine
Among children, throwing off the dream.
And power trips, and self-obliterating ideas
And scent of recriminations. Yet another

Pedestrian in charge makes jams.
Being so over-sensitive, falling back asleep;
Guilt about sanitary habits such as
The person who wishes you dead

When one doesn't manage to do anything
Out of the chair facing the cooker
In the hotchpotch of aches in the corners
And irritating underwear. Often enough

To be clean and unblemished as a new advertisement,
That has been denied a citizen:
Other than imagining not having had enough
Of when one feels too old to do anything

About heads held upright by anyone,
By being what we are, especially heartedness
Of an infinity done over, sleep,
The semi-faint and shock blanking out.

A further, deeper breath of lapsing
Into oblivion. How to be swayed by
Swaying eyes disunited, blanking out to sleep
And sleep a second time again.

Your Body Is All

Your body is all angles and balances
Like my mind. The shape of you
Is silence where things are posed.
Such things as are heard of,
Imagined, but never seen, I touch
When I hold you inexpertly
Before you go in from the rain.
Then I am left with a maidenly rain
Inside me, and cannot tell
Which way is home.

Extract from an Essay on Love

Don Juan's not the man who makes love to women,
But one to whom women make love.
He holds onto his reason for as long as he can.
Don José in a rage, emphasising his uncontrollable temper,
Once, verging on madness,
Killed someone who cheated him in a card game.
Don't secretes secrets.
"Free was I born, and free will I die."
And to die triumphantly outside the *corrida*
Seems to be universal. They die as deeply in love,
To wander in the outlaw-infested mountains.

The Question

A hardy perennial – is it to leave no trace
    like fish through the water or birds through the air?
Often we become clad in its aura
    when least conscious of what we are wearing
    – deep in a letter from the far west,
    while the sunset spills through panes
    reaching our blue dress and the blue chair.
While it might well be lift-off, it is never the in-flight movie;
    though its anathema, ugliness, may be no easier to identify
    – chicken innards on the bitumen outside the restaurant
    kitchen door; car-parks it will be difficult
    to find a use for after the demise of cars,
    or offices where automated decisions
    are fodder for shredders – the waste of trees.
But out beyond progress, that host of phoenixes, the bush
    burning and renewing itself, partakes of the order
    we associate with this; and it is fitting
    not to interfere but to bury one's debris and the remnants,
    to unpile any stones one has piled together,
    and to fill up the holes one has scooped in the sand.

Perhaps it's a train called Ken,
    flowers in a vase on the doily in a saucer
    on the table on the carpet
    covering the parquet in the alcove.
To form chains or to break habits.
Anything you say it may use in evidence against you;
    establishing the laws of its being
    only that these may be broken – like a mirror
    whose reflections are invented.
It is five objects, rather than fifteen.

However, whilst admitting that it is to be imperceptible
in the landscape, to vanish into it
rather than to stand out against it,
there is also the ravishment of a child's pathetic
clockwork machine turned umber by exposure
– rust, and the becoming of a relic.
Brash silveriness and the shining fantasias of the Cadillac.
The details, the myriad man-made things:
the winder, the head-frame, the skip;
saucepan and thermos; the bellows,
the wheelbarrow and the churn.
As much in the learning of names
as in the appraisal of their entities –
appreciation of the jack-hammer, the spoon-tool,
and the Beehive sock-knitting machine.
Broken jalopies, like beetles unable to right themselves;
monuments to the inaccessibility of their differentials.
Something to be stumbled upon
rather than turned craftily on the approved wheel.
Its trunk pushes upwards through the oil-drum.
A sensation of surprise recognised.
The gap of light between buttocks and thighs
– or darkness – it is the well.

The Surrealist

I have my cars in the hand-bag.
This is my rag and its mummy.
These are my fluff drivers.
I bring tea in my fist,
And try to bite your leg off.

The zero is driving the car.
Alfalfa sits in a chair of bricks.
The fire-guard is his cage.
Mummy aero had two baby aeros.

I don't like the telephone's eyes.
The cheese is walking up the stairs.
I put cars in the stew, and books.
The horse-box is asleep in the cupboard.

I can get a tractor. Here it is.
No, that's a man.
And what does the man do?
Puts the wheel on.
And what does the man say?
Put it in the horse-box.
What does the man say to the tractor?
This is a gun. This is a hamburger.

Lyrics from *Imruil*

Where She Dismounted

Droppings like pepper-tree pods, these courtyards
Haunted by the white gazelle.
Place between here and there and there and here.

Nothing takes root now, nothing.
Only the sand may nibble these flagstones.
Vanity builds such effective monuments.

Look, as much as north wind covers
South wind reveals.
There is never enough sand.

One Who Slices Bitter Gourds

Friends who depart have their caravan routes
To keep them occupied.
Platitudes are all one may expect.

Patience is a virtue. Soothe the heart with tears.
Listen, I have wept patiently.
Where may I sleep among these ruins?

The pale thorn throws scant shade.
Even in the few hours left me.
The wind brings tears to the eyes.

Remote Caravanserai

Mother of Cloud, the maidenly rains
Drift westwards; to the east
An emaciated crone hoes the topsoil.

This is grief, the legendary, tears
Of desire for what is, after all,
Hardly lamentable: the wail
That greys a man's fine beard,
Drenches his girdle, rusts his sword.

Feasting the Girls

Idiocy! My camel sank to its knees,
Stabbed in a frenzy induced by the giggles.
My saddle was made their trophy. Well
May you blush, sir, just as I would,
Were I younger, teased with the meat,
Garlanded with tassels of fat. Delicious!

Pleiades

Plump eggs are nested in those litters
Few design to raid – as if they were
Stone cold or not for the asking
To be had whenever the hen and her brood
Go peckety over the vast dark yard.
Unaizaki threads the brilliants,
Taking care to match them all in order,
So they form a necklet. "Wear it
And feel feathery." Behind the screen
She shivers in her nightie. "Who?"

Ridge above Ridge

"Paws to yourself, please. What's so clever
In going on your belly beneath the goatskins,
Nosing for goods the ostrich buried?
I'll carry the lamp: when we're dazzled
You make the blunders, but who takes the risk?
The vixen. She has to drag her brush
To cover the traces. Don't play the fool
If you want me to do the same with the fringes
Of my cloak. What is out here
But dunes, and dunes more firm by far
Than any mounds a girl like me can offer?
And you still haven't told me what we're after."

Concerning the Midden

Rubbing the back of the hand
Against her belly, say, her feel
Is the same as recently plucked
Silk: tight is her grip,
Tighter than the well-suppled thongs
That fasten gourd cups.

On me her fingers; indulgent
Maggots. Coupling is
A business both obligatory and private:
Like picking one's teeth, almost.

The Late Riser

Only her lips bother with those questionable
Pronouncements that intensify
Us bores – it is her voice she minds:
Under her coaching it has learnt
To stroke the ear with the same tedium
As the lean hand displays
Stroking the lapdog: thus she draws
A blind across our apprehension
Like the membrane in a dog's eye. Matrons
Would impeach the immodesty
Of her dress; daughters
Its old-fashioned cut: both
Mothers and maidens are left to quibble
Among themselves. Hers is a vague
Couch where musk obliterates

Us. Each man considers himself
My vizir. I ask after their wives.
Gossip, it seems, is of no
Interest. Her shadow walks within her:
She must have man-talk.

Target Practice

At the back of the dune she insists
It was no rendezvous: a grain
Manages to aggravate the silence.

Nor may my voice be correctly pitched
When the waste is all ear.
"At least let us say our goodbyes."

What makes her hoard my heart,
When my behaviour may be accounted for
By a distinct sense of loss?

Of no use now to its rightful owner;
Setting itself by her wrist.
"These tears only worsen the calamity."

Orientations

Inhaling the wind out of the east
One can tell it has satisfied
The camphor leaves. "Bring
Me a gift with nothing in your hands.

Be adorned with bruises for broaches,
Shadows that cling for a while
When bracelets anklets etceteras are removed:
Your simple waist swayed by a breeze."

One may gaze into her breast longer
Than one can into the smoothest
Mirror. What feeds such a phenomenon?
Water, when it is thin and clear.

A Night's Peace

When it is their wives who run
To catechize my management
Then there is something to answer for.

Soon such torrential bitterness
May turn to brine
That river which is simply a place to drown.

Stars are a foam on its surface:
Into it we sink forever,
Deeply committed, like pebbles.

The Lord of Rule

Night provides a brute
That is the night:
He buttocks with his buttocks.

The moon, trussed up despite
Her clucking,
Hangs across his saddle-pegs.

Tethered to the hill,
His planets graze no further afield
Than their ropes allow.

Before whose might prostrate myself?
You or this afflicted prince
Terrorized by morning?

The Comparison

To lay one's head between
His shoulders, deep
In his mane.

Sweeter than being
Pestle and mortar
Held between virgin knees

About a young bride
Is the slightly off-putting
Incense of possession.

His Fierce Dressage

"Seraph, though you were capable of
Most scholarly equitation
When you were bitted: shoulderings in,
Changes of leg and caprioles
That outdid the Jew for piety,
I doubt you were even wildly tame.
Rashly once I turned you loose:
It took five days for me you and
The appropriate corner to coincide.
Saddled, but with girth unstrung,
Jealously guarding your rear,
You rolled the dark white marbles in
Your bridled face – though fast asleep."

The Well-Tempered Stallion

1

Long before the first hour to be lit,
While every nest kept its occupants
Huddled mute, I used to exercise
That horse. Now at his loins a touch
Would inform him to wheel,
Though not long before I found him proud,
Foaming his flanks in the wild.

Soon enough I had him schooled:
He was a stone abducted by the spate;
Polished by my impulsion till
The saddle-cloth slid off his back.
I was diligent as a cloth
Of water, varnishing a stone.

2

Then I dissolved in him, mingled mine
With his blood – hastiness
Sustained: arrogant rapids thundering past
Numb banks where swept-back predators
Stuck in their leap, tethered
To a formal ranting, as in a frieze.

We squealed, we showed the dust
Our hooves, refused
A bridge if a gorge were offered;
Rolled in none but the thorny places,
Farting if aroused, and ours
A fart bellicose as the meat-pot's.

Like a Hyena-Bone Top

Child's play to ride – although his swivelling
Giddied those uninitiated
Pedestrians who hoped to buy
Their seat. Such corpulent eunuchs these,
He smothered them in their cloaks.

Child's play – but the shifty child
Unceremoniously thrown:
A light-weight missile, should he release,
Accurate as a sling, his buck.

His Affinities

Hyenas may be congratulated
On nothing but their stamina:
My lord adopted that lope
And the to-and-fro walk
Of the wild dog, also
The fox's jog, and other gaits.

But his quarters were completely
A gazelle's, his kick
That of the ostrich's thin leg,
And the hair of his tail
Pure horse.

3

Privity

Lately the sun oozes through, the gorse perseveres,
Despite a sodden resemblance to a sea-floor,
The pussy dust is a brilliant sprinkled yellow,
While the oaks disencumber their arms.

Insectless anthers of snowdrop and crocus
Practise autogamies available to such early birds,
As also to declining flowers, capable
On emergence of cross-pollination only:

A method for the self-enclosed, the unopening,
The cut-off plants, in the wilderness,
Like the *Salvia:* small, solitary,
Odourless and unvisited as the knot-grass.

Out Together

It's quite a walk to where a bridge and stile
Straddle the Hart, at the edge of Hartley Wintney:
Getting there eventually, the body loosens;
Ease pervades the legs, the trunk,
The arms leaning against its rudimentary balustrade,
With a foot up against the lower bar.
We peer down at the weeds, and Quixotic tilts
Prang obviously as the rushes ebb
From the mind's reaches. Musings turn
To other matters. Here, at least for a while,
The brook wriggles across a water-meadow,
Dogs wag after water-rats holed in the bank's
Precipice, and the child babbles up
From beneath. "Where does it go,
The little river? What have the dogs seen, Daddy?"
After a breather, there are the pigs
To see, and the sewage farm and the dump.
This last being Mecca for practical purposes;
Dragging a small arm or carrying
A lump dangling gumboots across a heath.

A Young Mother

She was weighed down by the one child;
Weighed down by the arms. Too old
For a piggy-back, they pull the shoulders
Out of their sockets. On the cover
Of a book women pulled at a rope.

The waiter set down a Martini.
They get set down and forgotten about
Or snatched up so that their handles rip.
She had forgotten to ring the station.
Her mother-in-law snatched up her son
Whose pants had ripped on a fence.
Either they come free or you have
To pay for them. Just then her eyelash
Came free of the lid. She was told
She would have to pay for the operation.
Bags carrying precious objects or perfume
Can be used again for the garbage.
Saint Christopher carried his load.
She wondered whether her body ever would
Be used again, the child weighed.

Lead Soldiers

They tended to snap at the ankles,
And now they are things of the past:
Hollow amputees in boxes
Buried under cards from scattered
Happy Family packs; sans appeal
To kids in plastic macs
Dragging their mums along flexible fences
Coated like flex while this token father
Crosses the bitumen playground to a hut.
Yes, it's an age of plastics: bibs and trucks,
Bricks, helmets, bren-guns.
His son plays with a road-roller
In tea-leaves kept on a vinyl tray.

Everyone gets milk, their own plastic bottle,
And a ditto biscuit. And there's
A slide, a vacu-formed marina –
Then there's the sandpit with buckets
And moulds for castles. And they make pictures
With blue macaroni, perspex buttons
And the spongy nuggets of styrofoam
Used to fill out cavities in packing-cases.
"Not up her nose!"

And that night it's the red plastic
Sea-horse, the globe with rocking horses
And a one-time rocking swan, the paddle
Of a deep-sea fishing vessel, deconstructed
To the last rowlock – and a sort of
Bridge of slats for soap across the bath.

Maintenance

Despite peacock butterflies plastered
Onto flowering teasels, every day of the week
Produces a storm, this miserable summer.
The buddleia is blasted, nettles drown a fence,
Deck-chair mattresses crumple, shot in the groin,
As emerald bugs crawl slowly through the mint.
Nobody swims – the pool shows a green tinge
Which calls you out to scatter crystals
And activate the filter. No reflection garnishes
The vague, still water. A residue of algae
Forms on the bottom in sand-like drifts.
Absently watching the next cloud over

Dull the transient brightness of a field,
You note another flaw in your submission
Minutes after the envelope has been sealed.
These corrections never get you anywhere,
And perpetual treading water is a destiny
That only puts a spoke in your career.
Rejecting the fruit of labours entertains
Like suicide, but the clouded surface below
Refuses to accept a soon-to-be-discarded
Version of you hoovering the unfrequented pool.

Splices

Rejected Plains Indians pretend with a horse in drag.
My uncle's was the first I went to, dressed as a page
In velvet. Fun conducting the organ from
Behind the bridal train. Kept the pews in stitches,

Though my uncle disapproved.
Blackfoot wedding guns get fired
On the day of the mudbrick lampbulb. Uncle's bride
Used relic oil that year of camera dread.

I bumped into her gourd voice-disguiser.
That was a hoot. Mother kept recalling it,
Much to my embarrassment. Seemed to lack decorum:
The Blood Indians in their bicycle-chain blue jeans.

Next was the grand union of the Mozambique pianos.
Everyone came to their breakfast.
We got hitched ourselves dangling from fishing-rods
Above the cottage roof. Now that was a high point.

A marionette at the registry pronounced us what we were,
While Marvin wolfed the buffet: he was my best man
– A Coney Island comic, punishing the pun,
While you swanned around with a red dress on.

Land commissioners in pith helmets met crocodiles
In straw hulas. All my relatives accepted
The hash cookies. I barged into your sister
Changing into less decorous attire. I kissed her.

Meanwhile the dog had finished off the cookies.
Later I came across her looking bemused.
Slowly all four legs slid away from each other.
Then she went to my mother's car to be sick.

Nudes

Slow is the heart
To love what the eye cannot see.
The watcher notes the eternal light
Within the watched, the mortal being.
Great longing the only experience
Experienced under the warm white light:
The nude strolling, taut backs
Of the spirit knees
And stocky beginnings of calves.

Wonder of how things fit
Or are soft enough to permit us in there.
Nests of removable arms
Along the limbs, between bells.
Amphorae, shells, anemones.
Coverts and enclosures
Looking inward on themselves.
Their privacy is thus their protection.
The grapes seem swollen with light.

The Age of the Street

Here is the passing of an uneventful hour
In a backwater of the town, above a backwater of the bay
Behind the containers brought to this faraway shore.
Wall-to-wall carpet, sweet-smelling dust in the air,
The gloss of doors, each knob a scintilla of day,
Rackets and hats, glimpses of sash and pane
Through the blinds, flaws troubling the picture-plane:
Then lengths of railing, kerb and the grey camber
Levelling off into gutters lead the eye away
With the newsboy's whistle as he tugs his trolley of papers
Up the shallow incline punctuated by some blooms.
An hour between darkness and light for overcast portions
Of changeable afternoons; monochrome, khaki and amber
Moments with no more definition than a reproduction
In the discarded volume: vacant chairs and rooms,
Reticent gardens, phones unanswered, pasted-over heaven,
Locked factory gates. The blinds obey the suction
Or suspension of the breeze, exhale or hold their breath in;
Blinds gathered up or closing jerkily to obliterate

The criss-cross canvas view permitted through a mosquito net
Gridding the surface – before, or exhausted after
A storm out of season, watched through the slits in Venetians.
A print smears the sheen of dust on an outer wing,
The texture of macadam alters, rain or shine,
As wobbly birds with a few feathers begin to sing
Wibbly-wobbly songs, and a weeping willow caresses
A Volkswagen in the otherwise uninhabited street.
Then a motorbike, or a girl casually shouldering tresses
Turns the corner, hardly in sight before gone
Past fronts incurious as to whether prompt or late.
Thinnish cloud, inconsequential wind, a sagging wire,
While a bit of colour is provided by the parked car.
Here, what's on the air is just preferred a little softer:
Loud noise-makers are locked behind factory gates.
Different hours obtain for dogs than do for cats.
Across the bay there's a stillness about the black lifter.

Groves of Academe

My darlings wet from the bushes,
Girls the intense times I have:
Your junction of branches, squidge
Of buttocks, peeling of nylons;
The tremor inside pantaloons
Or curve revealed as a T-shirt
Bends towards the seeded plot,
Or half in a bath and drying off.
My poem is broken up with love.
Missing it gives me the lean,
Hungry look of a visiting lecturer.

Reclining Figure

Woman, lie still and tan,
Loath to disturb ubiquitous sand
With its stone mash and its shell meal
Getting into the nap of towels
And with a grain
Spoiling the smooth rub of an oiled palm.

Love Poem

I have tried to write you a love poem,
But its reasoning doesn't ring true:
Shouldn't it imply a belief in something,
Sex for instance, not to mention you.

Undermining belief in anything
There's the work of those talented moderns
Who begin from nothing. Certainly I find it
More sensible to be writing you a letter

Rather than a love poem. In a love poem
There seems to me a conflict between
a) the desire to communicate and b)
The compulsion to make a thing of beauty.

The beauty of the poem is a rival to the beauty
Of the person. It purports to be about them
But is only interested in drawing attention to itself:
A reason for rejecting the poet who wrote it.

Beauties loved by poets get irritated
When they receive poems dedicated to them.
This may not deter the adolescent who
Thinks that a poem can win love by its eloquence

– Which it invariably fails to do.
Given it could, the person probably
Likes you enough anyway to go to bed with you.
Pen and ink will simply delay matters.

Can such poetry only be a projection
Onto an unknown and not particularly loving quantity?
I wanted then, if not to write a love poem,
To create a written version of a life-drawing

Or a well-oiled painting choc-a-bloc with bodies
Like 'The Death of Sardanapalus'.
Here the carnage apposite to his last throes
Infringes upon shared intimacy though;

And I remain uncomfortably aware
That some readers may not be so taken by it.
One man's meat, Erotica never gets through
To everybody – as Literature ought to.

I have tried to write you a love poem,
But there's altogether too much intended
For even an abstract, collaged attempt
Not to betray my brand of mental weakness.

Either form or content reads askew;
Yet there persists a prior image of the love poem
One day one might write
Which coaxes me to have another go at it.

Eating One's Cake

There's no place like us. Home is not family.
I love my son, and I love your legs, your bum.
If I'm in my native country but not in your arms
Then I'm abroad so far as I'm concerned.

No sad sacrifice of desire for responsibility.
Debts are less than pleasant – pleasure is the bond.
The lane down to the Hampshire farm, bordered
With bracken and brambles is more foreign than

Making it with you in some unlikely room.
The boy calling me dad may show me his treasures.
But without the certainty of being inside you again ,
I can take little joy in his ash-tree stage-coach,

Dead elm space-ship, galleon of a toppled fir.
Properly bedded, I am wherever you are,
Our *heimat* our pretend distress and cruelty,
As I use what I want of you and you of me.

Should good behaviour smother self-direction?
Must separation always preclude further friendship?
Why choose between glum versions of happiness:
Decency's drudgery versus a loose burning

The candle at both ends? There are better ways
Of working things out than opting for either
Being stuffed down the bosom of the norm
Or slung out of it on an expressionist fling.

Home is my own being centred on itself.
I get there by sorting things out as they are,
Not as they seem to others. For my own reasons
Rather than for some view of correctness

Or taken-up advice. As personal as a door-key,
The answer negotiates one specific lock,
Swings open under my own roof, where and when
I can smile my smile, entirely contented to be me.

Aftermath

All the stupendous canopies are on the wane.
You let the cloud fall down onto your lap in the afternoon.
Fondle the creature. She is very nice to touch.
Lift her breasts up. Forceps. Convulsive wind-swells.

Last night had been more or less a complete disaster.
Fate hung in the air, its reverberations
Louder than a fly-past. They had forgotten to refer
To the Tide Tables. Treacherous local onshores.

"She just threw herself. And naturally I was flattered."
Hiatus of broken glass, corrugated sheets, rusted girders,
Wedges of concrete, soiled soil and cinders.
"I want to get down the bowels of your trunk."

In the silence we pick up the pieces – a smashed brief-case,
The rear window back there in the bull dust,
The corkscrewed exhaust. Mange affects yellow grasses,
Motionless hawk spirals above the tracks

Where we wait later, motionless ourselves among
Antiquated phones and ticket dispensers. Motionless also
Are the men on the platform against sacks of oranges.
The train takes us past dead cars, vineyards.

Idea of the South

It seems a planet composed entirely of atmosphere
    with nothing in it but a few incredible cloud formations.
The spacious sky bears unforeseeable weather
    in eddies and whirlpools under the pole at its base.

A centrifugal force thrusts what land there is
    to far-flung margins. Affected more by the tides
Than ever by seasons, life clings to the atolls
    or crowds the horse-shoe rims of dried-up seas.

Chains of volcanoes go off, one after another,
    where oceans crack, and where the crust holds firm
Five o'clock shadow forms on a place so extensive
    that somewhere inside it there's always a sunset.

Weather, with its maddening and exhilarating waywardness,
    douses a drought, evaporates flood with fire.
Archers and dogs, crosses and scorpions, ladders and snakes
    litter the Milky Way till out of the picture.

Many of the stars are upside-down or back-to-front;
Orion looks as if he had met with an accident,
The moon tilts, man stares down on his maker:
above his feet is a world that's the right way up.

By day the wind sallies forth into the desert,
coming at night to cool the waves offshore.
Surf around the coast is merely a reflection
of cyclones afar whirling around like dervishes.

Rain dins from a height on Southern plains:
the appropriate scale is a size or two larger than life.
Boys outgrow their first generation fathers;
pre-fab extensions trespass over the gardens.

Inland, the stations are like orb-spiders' webs:
they radiate strands of rusting windswept wire.
Koalas drift the hillsides in search of specific gums;
nomadic birds commute between nesting and feeding grounds.

A blackfellow's walkabout becomes an Odyssey.
The natural pace of thought is a slow meander.
Visiting the dentist or going out to a film
can mean a five-hour car ride, or an aeroplane.

In the harbours of this hemisphere containers
package whole lives, pasts as yet unloaded, labelled
For destinations only reached by road-trains
pulled along by lorries larger than houses.

They roll to a standstill in deserted towns
with upper verandahs overlooking the mulga,
Or halt at bushwhacked blocks with letterbox churns
on desolate ridges or chasms far from the highway.

Truck-stops where tame wallabies eat the stubs
    out of spittoons, or where some recent owner
Has been found attached to a car-battery in the creek.
    A land which can't be known 'like the back of a hand',

With so few lines on its palm it suggests the mystery
    of what mirrors reflect in our absence.
Dish-white flats where rocks like very large hard-boiled eggs
    roll into shape without witnesses.

Keeping on hold that pandemonium in the aisles
    where guano gets recycled onto the peck-gutter,
Something persists of the South before its discovery,
    when maps baulked at the odd landfall

Which kept cropping up on the wrong bearings;
    when the contours of supposed territories failed to connect,
Disappearing into the herbaceous border of nimbus.
    This is the South where time seeps out of our watches.

Hints of affray may be discerned in the windows
    of homes hidden by the reflection of the sky,
But human presence is only a phenomenon at the edges,
    where immigrant poplars hardly know which way to turn.

Coral islands with monuments erected by Byron
    to kings and queens who died of the measles in London;
While beige memorials to its dun-coloured troops
    clutter this flyblown, out-of-mind establishment.

It could be no better concocted by Raymond Roussel
    from aboriginal tongue-twisters, put together
In a closed carriage rattling across the Gibson:
    trees made entirely from creeper, living Gaudis,

Prairies prohibited by cliff-walls, reservoirs of silence,
    manifestations of elemental powers, torrents
Of specific energies, nights of masonic symbol.
    This is the refuge of the Sacred Ibis.

Last moment footage fades the departure lounge
    into a wind-wheel fanned by the sunset,
Blurring its vanes in a land neither dead nor alive
    on a planet half dazzle, half drizzle and twilight.

4

Boxing the Cleveland

Boxing the Cleveland

A coach-built lorry, several metres long,
Is backing down the grass-bound lane between
The weather-boarded shack where clothes are hung
And that old shed for wood. The lane leads on

Past chicken-runs behind a criss-cross fence
On the woodshed side, beyond the much-decayed
Remains of a kennel, overgrown with dense
Nettles and docks, and then on past those frayed

Rails the horses gnaw through the winter, bordering
The sunset paddock, there on the laundry side.
The lane is closed by a new gate worth the ordering
With its lightweight bars on which the children ride

At the downhill end, and by one painted white,
Which is seldom used but can be pulled across
At the end where the ground increases in height
Towards those sheds behind the red-brick house.

The lorry's box is partitioned for at least
Four horses standing sideways in their stalls:
Its width permits a squeezing space at best
Between its sides and the nettle-bordered walls

Hard by the lane, where it's brought to a juddering stop
Beside the gate pushed back against the shed
Serving as laundry. Someone thin on top
Comes out of the house and greets with nod of head

The woman who switches the engine off, a breaker
Aged about thirty, dressed in jodhpurs, who lands
On the ground while a girl and a woman like her
Climb from the passenger side – her helping hands.

The three squeeze past the gate-posts into the lane;
Then rattles, thuds and hammer-blows are heard
As round the back the ramp is lowered, then
Its side-gates and its uprights get secured,

And a well-stuffed hay-net's hung inside the stall
At the ramp's head there, in readiness for the horse.
Quick swallows flit the sheds. It's early still
On a summer's evening. Horses crop the grass

Below a sky of livid, swirling veils
Auguring storms. The atmosphere is close.
The breaker woman clambers through the rails,
And in between the thistle-clumps she goes,

Holding a lunge. She's back inside a minute,
Leading a four-year-old, prancing, tossing his head
In its halter, fretfully stalling and fighting agin it,
But out of the sunset firmly and forcefully led.

There's a fine horse: a colossal Cleveland Bay
Bearing aloft his Roman nose, his ears
Pricked forwards as he strides, then sidles shy
Of an elder bush. He snorts now, as he nears

The horse-box, ill-disposed to walk in hand.
Unshod, as yet unbroken, how he towers
Above the woman eager to command
Obedience, however many hours

It takes to do it. Now she lays her stick
Against his neck and pulls him while his shank
Precedes the older woman who will flick
His quarters should he baulk, and at his flank

A smallish man in mackintosh and cap:
Together with the girl who shakes the pail,
This makes a team resolved he will go up
Inside the box – determined not to fail –

While he who came directly from the house
Decides to watch the struggle, not engage
In any sort of help beyond advice,
Or that is how he sees it at this stage.

At first the Cleveland halts to sniff the ramp;
The second time he brings a hoof to pound it,
Striking more than once to test his stamp,
And blowing dirt, his large head firmly grounded.

The woman breaker hauls him up again,
While those behind him offer him no leisure:
Pushing, prodding, beating him between
Hocks and haunches, they increase the pressure.

'Just keep niggling with the whip, Jane,
Rather than waving it wildly like that. Go on,
Go on,' the woman says. She tugs the rein,
Her hands in gloves to guard against a burn.

'Come on, Sweetheart, it'll be nicer in here:
No flies.' The flies outside enjoy the sweat
Of brute and human; crawl within each ear,
Or else beneath his loins – they make him fret

And whisk his tail. A shudder shakes his frame.
'Isn't the slope too steep for him, Miranda?'
Her looker-on has never caught her name.
Only a fool spectator would demand her

Answer. 'Lead him from a distance to it.
That way he approaches straight, Miranda.
Mind you, if he doesn't want to do it
That'll be that – one never can command a

Horse that big by sheer brute force.' 'He can't
Be given the chance of going back,' she says.
'But he's in a panic.' My God, what an aunt
Of a man to one who knows her Cleveland Bays.

'He's not in a panic. Why should he be?' she smiles.
'He's stubborn, so we'll cut him down to size.'
Of course the ramp is far too steep for heels.
But will the woman listen to advice?

'You'll never fight him up the ramp, Miranda.'
'My name's Virginia – and I'll get him there.'
Why should she give up? Her motto is never surrender.
With burning ears, the man might now retire

But stays to help. 'Good boy, that's right, good man!
Let's place his off-forehoof against the ramp
– Don't try to lift it, push him off it, then
He'll use the other foot, but watch his jump.

Come on, Petrushka! Rattle the nuts at him, Mary.
Don't let him have them – not until he's in.
Haven't we got any real nuts in the lorry
Other than grass-nuts? Mary, try the bin.

Hoi, you, don't push at me! How dare
You barge like that?' She whacks him on the jaw.
Changing her tactics, should he stand and stare,
She bullies him, or coaxes as before:

'There's a good horse! Try lifting his foot again.'
The smaller man encourages his wary
Movement forwards, punishing him when
His hooves recant – for being so contrary.

Fond words, and a thrashing when they fail:
The ramp becomes that terror of the brink.
Lead a horse to water, shake the pail,
But can you get him boxed or make him drink?

'Get behind him, Jane, it's just no use
Slashing at him from the front like that:
It makes him more determined to refuse.
Upset him, and we could be here all night.'

By now she can expect to pull him round
Back to the ramp's edge if and when she pleases;
Even force his forefeet off the ground
Onto the ramp – but this is where he freezes.

The trouble is the lane: its downward cant
Is yet another factor for each hoof
To cope with: since the ramp is at a slant,
This incline makes it steeper than a roof.

And what about the box? Of poor design,
That gap between its ramp-hinge and its floor
Creates a step – eight inches, maybe nine –
And here's a horse who's not been boxed before;

A gangling sixteen hands with much to learn;
Who jibs against the rein with lengthened neck
And drags behind. At grass since he was born,
He's yet to feel a saddle touch his back.

As darkness falls, the towering sky releases
Spatterings of rain by fits and starts:
The risk of slipping down the ramp increases.
Buttocks bared, the Cleveland stales and farts

Whenever half-way up it, looking stilted:
Leaning from his stubborn rear, he stretches,
Craning his neck out; whiffles at the tilted
Surface with his lips and nostrils, reaches

Forwards for that tantalising pail
Of pony nuts, and rising 'on his toes'
He teeters off his haunches – can he fail
To reach the treat one inch before his nose?

A hindhoof rests on edge – he's not prepared
To place it on the ramp though: once or twice
He's put it there before – but now he's scared
Of slipping on its rubber mat, because

Whenever he puts weight on it, the hoof
Slides from beneath him. Were he just to walk
Straight up the ramp collected he'd be safe,
But at full stretch, on rubber, with his bulk

Above his forelegs, forward moving these
More often than his stern, he comes unstuck
And flounders badly, stumbles to his knees,
To scramble his reversal, bruise a hock

Against an edge and yank his hapless breaker
Out of the box now, fighting to maintain
Her grip on him. And when he fails to make her
Let him go, he drags her down the lane,

Wrenching her elbows; scattering all as he battles,
Hauling her after him headlong into the bush
There by the woodshed, through those vicious nettles,
In a back-off only halted by the mesh

Which fences in the chicken-runs, and then
Bouncing his rear against it, blowing hard.
The woman pulls his muzzle round again,
But now he can't be got within a yard

Of where the ramp comes down across the lane
Without a good hard slash to sting his arse
Back into action – 'Keep him moving, Jane.
You're going to learn who's boss, you bloody horse.

I don't care if we're here till four o'clock
Tomorrow morning.' 'Come on, come on, ay,'
The flat-capped fellow coaxes, as they rock
The horse's quarters forwards. 'That's the way.'

'I want it set up so he can't reverse,'
The breaker says. 'Try bringing both the whips
Behind him now.' No better, if no worse,
He gets so far, and then he locks his hips.

'Try Push-me-pull-you: while I pull, you push.
Get your head up, get it up, d'you hear?
Do you, do you?' Giving him a bash,
Virginia is at pains to make it clear

The fight is far from over. All the same,
She says inside her shirt she's sopping wet
And grins at that – a lather-making game
For horses too though, judging by his coat.

The man with thinning hair attempts to put
His shoe-cap through the ramp-foot's metal ring –
One of the pair on which it's meant to sit
But rides askew on, causing quite a bang

Whenever she walks up it, horse in tow.
By bearing down one keeps the ramp-edge flush
With what's beneath it. There, it's better now;
No bang to send him backwards in a rush.

This makes an ounce of difference to initial
Moments, as the Cleveland follows on:
But such improvement soon looks superficial.
He will not go beyond where he has gone.

'I'm sure it's far too steep.' 'It isn't though,'
The woman says, 'He's just determined not to.'
(Why should she heed a man who doesn't know?)
'He'll do it, now he's got to where he's got to.

What happens here could prove the most significant
Event in all his breaking,' she insists.
'With proper schooling he could be magnificent,
But he'll be useless if he once resists

And finds he has the strength to get away with it.
He has to learn it isn't all in fun.
I tell you now, to wait another day with it
Would set him back. I mean to get it done.'

And now the other horses take to galloping
About the paddock, spinning him around.
'Do that again, I'll give you such a walloping
You won't forget it! Please don't walk around

Him while he's on the ramp. It just distracts
From what we're trying to do.' The breaker vents
Her spleen on someone watching who reacts
By keeping still behind a distant fence.

'Let's keep trying. Can you bear it? Good.
Petrushka, you come in, don't toss your mane.
The world could be your oyster if you would.'
How poached the ground along the darkened lane.

He's laced in froth, the woman hot and dirty,
Yet relentless; not a single break
From ten-to-six till past eleven-thirty:
A glass of water all she cares to take.

Tempted, wheedled, bullied, given stick,
That horse remains as bloody-minded now
As when they started – rearing up and back
Before the sky; a threat to those below,

His forefeet scrape the clouds, he topples over on
His haunches, crashes down against the rail,
The ramp-gates or the nettles or the chicken-run,
And rears afresh – takes all the rein – to flail

For balance, but he loses it and sprawls
Across the ramp, then rolls right through the bush;
And far too green to know quite how one falls,
He thrashes on his back like any fish

Flung gasping on the bank. He hates the line.
Again he rears, and now the lunge-rein snaps,
Or else he wheels and knocks the woman down,
And as she falls each flustered chicken flaps

And squawks behind the fence. He gallops over her
With hooves aflurry through the battered nettles:
Curled with covered ears, what hardly bothers her
Except for stings most certainly unsettles

Those who help. She rises to her feet
Before the others reach her. Someone goes
To hold the tossing horse. 'Are you alright?'
At least Petrushka keeps her on her toes.

The flat-capped man removes his mac;
The woman with the whip is losing heart;
The rattling of pony nuts goes slack;
But the nettle-prickled breaker wants to start

That Cleveland up the ramp again, although
Her jodhpurs have been stained from where he churned
Her briefly in the stingers. As from now,
He'll do it in a bridle – as she warned

The owner he might have to, since the halter
Will not hold him. Sheer determination
Gets the head-piece done without a falter,
Then he flings his head in consternation

Out of reach and shakes it. Most unsure,
He pauses near the lower gate to dung.
She manages to grab him by the jaw
And slip the snaffle-bit across his tongue.

She then secures the cheek-piece to its ring,
Fastens up the throat-lash, and he's ready.
Right away, it's far less work to bring
Him back towards the ramp. 'Now keep it steady.'

Things go better. Never by enough
To get him up the incline, home and dry.
'I'll take a cigarette. My word, he's rough,'
The smaller man says. Then once more they try

To shift his shoulders, bend him at the knee
And place his hoof some distance up the ramp.
'Take care he don't come down on you,' says he.
' 'Cause if he did he'd land a fair old bump.'

And later, with the only light one dim
Effulgence from the box, before the chap
With thinning hair can quite manuvre him
Another step, and thus prevent a slip

By hauling him across the rubber mat,
And making certain that his hoof is brought
In contact with an elevated slat
To give him purchase, should he bring his weight

To bear upon it, up he goes, and down
He crashes on the man who promptly buckles,
Trapped beneath his girth, and duly thrown
Against the gate to smart among the prickles.

The smaller fellow pushes back his cap:
'If you reversed the lorry, so's the ramp
Fell open down the slope, we'd get him up.
He'd find it all downhill, and then the chump

Would feel as he was walking back towards
The other horses; now he must presume
He's leaving them behind. In other words,
We'd get him if he wasn't leaving home.

And if we close the upper gate as well,
And park the box just several paces, say,
Along the lane and very near the wall,
He wouldn't have the space to pull away.'

A dozen times already, that big horse
Has bolted from his handlers down the lane,
Has left them sitting straddled there to curse
The nettles, or he's torn away the rein

And galloped off towards his native premises,
To stand and toss his head above the gate;
Only to be brought back to his Nemesis
Beneath the moon, behind a four-horse crate.

Virginia is his Atropos. 'Don't think
You can just stand there, old son,' she says, giving
The rein a yank if he pauses too long at the brink
Of the ramp. 'Till you're in, life's not worth living.

Push-me-pull-you again, Jane. Up you come.'
And again the Cleveland slashes down at the ramp
With an unshod hoof to clang the slats and drum
The rubber mat there, shining smooth and damp.

'Get your head up, get it up, you brute!'
The strain begins to show – his one desire
To end it all, to fold away his feet.
No longer can the pony nuts inspire

An edging forwards; only fear of hurt,
When those who grit their teeth increase the force
Of their persuasions, brings him back alert,
Eyes rolling, ears laid back: a nervous horse

Out of whose foam-flecked mouth the bit will slide
When pulled upon, and though he loathes the thing,
And shakes his bridled head from side to side,
That bar of steel remains beside his tongue

And pulls him wheresoever she sees fit.
He follows willy-nilly – till she brings
Him near the ramp. She loosens off the bit
To double-pass her lunge-rein through the rings

And get a surer purchase on his head.
But even so, misgivings make him baulk.
There comes a time when one will not be led,
And further up the ramp he will not walk,

Although it grieves his tongue to so recoil.
He droops, his jaw agape, his weary length
Stretched out and up the ramp, resolved to fail,
With heaving sides, and hardly any strength

To carry on the struggle. Swollen pink,
His aching tongue lolls out between his lips.
With flattened ears, he stands in utter funk
Below the woman. Desultory drops

Are falling now. The one who's going bald
Suggests they put a carpet down below
His hooves to make the incline more a slide;
And while Virginia likes to run the show,

She doesn't take much urging to endorse
A paint-stained piece of carpet for its floor;
But this strange item only fills the horse
With more distrust, he backs away the more

And backs away again. To keep him calm,
They lay aside the carpet till at least
He has his forelegs squarely on the climb,
And then they spread the carpet out as best

They can beneath his belly, where it can't
Be seen by him, though offering a sound
Foundation should he trust the upward slant
To trepidatious heels and quit the ground.

Virginia makes a noise by sucking air
Through puckered lips, as if she begged a kiss.
'Get in there,' says the man with thinning hair,
His shoulder to the horse's quarters. This

Is never going to budge him, so the whip
Is used to loop a line behind his tail
Which is tightened while the fellow in the cap
Lifts a fetlock to that rattle from the pail.

But nothing works. They might as well try out
The change suggested by that smaller man:
The lorry's driven forwards and about
The turning circle, then towards the lane.

The Cleveland ambles past, perhaps in hope
That this ordeal is over, it's so late;
But now the lorry faces down the slope,
A yard or so beyond the upper gate.

Then once again the ramp is rattled down
And fitted with its uprights as before.
Again the horse is brought inside the lane,
The white gate swinging shut behind his rear.

It's after ten, and very dark by now
– The only light that feeble glow inside
The box, although the stars put on a show
Of pricked-out constellations where they ride

Between the fewer clouds. The balding man
Walks over to the cars parked cheek by jowl
Beside the barn. He gets into his own
And starts the engine. Once he hears it growl,

He flicks the beams undipped, reverses clear,
Then gently rolls towards the upper gate.
His head-lamps give the light which they require:
Twin incandescent discs illuminate

The horse's rump, the jodhpurs and the rein,
The girl who shakes her pail within the tall
Entrance to the box, the flat-capped man,
The woman with her whip, the waiting stall,

And then the hay-net, hanging from its hook
Untouched as yet. Partitions open wide,
In order that the naïve horse may look
Beyond the stall and sense the depth inside.

The man who runs his motor feels content
To contemplate their progress from his wheel.
But soon it proves unpleasant to prevent
Obscurity – his engine starts to smell;

And if he switches off but leaves the lights on
He'll never get the car to start again.
It really makes no difference if she fights on
In the darkness, says the woman at the rein.

He kills the headlamps; goes inside to eat.
And by the time he wanders back to check,
The boxing of the Cleveland is complete.
He's feeding, while the women pat his neck

Inside his stall. He gets a good rub-down.
The ramp is raised. Virginia climbs aboard
And backs the lorry through the gate, to turn
And drive away with scarce another word.

Now that should be the end of that; however,
Late next afternoon both horse and box
Are back again: and it's as if they'd never
Been away. The breaker woman walks

Only with great difficulty though:
She had no problem getting home alright,
But then Petrushka did not care to go
Head first, descending, down into the night.

Instead, he felt decidedly installed,
And when she tried coercion, out he lashed
And caught her on the thigh, and so rebelled
Her stable girl got well and truly squashed.

So there he had to stay, since they were spent.
Tomorrow they would try a different tack.
But daylight failed to budge him, and he went
To some grand show beside her well-schooled hack

Who looked askance at one who never left
His stall to win a heat. Quite sans rosette,
He loitered in the lorry, though bereft
Of food and drink. He wasn't leaving yet.

The massive lorry faces down the hill
Inside the sunset paddock, opened wide
Among familiar horses: will he still
Refuse to take that necessary slide?

Out clatters he, his Roman nose held high,
No sooner than the ramp has touched the ground.
And ruefully the woman laughs to see
Him whisking his disdainful tail around

And striding off. But though he's got her foxed,
And though he gave her thigh-bone such a crack,
And though he strolls unbroken, he's been boxed
– And though he may not know it, she'll be back.

5

Nuova Austin Montego

After half the night waiting in front
Of the station, we step up onto corrugated
Rubber over grids, reaching for rods
And hand-holders. Do not obstruct
Several Australian Francescas with packs,
Inside-out socks and maps falling apart.
Our bus of birds careers past the Playboy
Beltrami duomo, the back of its Gucci
Mountain, a blue light on and off
The Tango pizzeria and a white string vest.

Yellow eyes of lions – indifferent
And dangerous. Without human emotion.
Incurious. Unblinking. Direct.
"I did *not* like that lift." "What a jerk!"

Driving to Cuma

Off we go, through a land with nothing on:
Dry beds, the sun beating all colour
From its carpet, space-age water towers,
A red car overtaking a black car,
Then SOSs, yellow grass and butterflies
Before tunnels – or cancer in the eyes.
We drink fizz from a source out of a bottle.
A house without walls between each floor
Stems from its roof-supports, like a Giotto.
Was that a playground in the cemetery
For the little children of Saturnia?
A zebra bends red walls round lava hotels;
Past dusty gum trees and a broken Lancia.

Thunder, Vesuvius, thunder. Rustle of heat.
Small tongue of a bird outside the vault.
The boy in the tree and a bird flying upwards.
Dark ripples of time in the shadows
Of leaves. Lovely dappling on the front
Of a girl with the face of an old man.

Primitive Colours

Her upright inky figure trims the glitter:
That blob stuck in the sand is a parasol.
Dazzle on spindrift glazes tearaway crests,
Blotting out foreground pitched at the intensity
Of a bay buttered gold. The girl in the Speedo
One-piece with cross-straps at the back
Steps out of the wet with a shiver. There
Goes a brown running boy. Choppy wavelets
Float gilded cornflakes on the brimming crater.
Black headland spills a tree-tossed silhouette,
And the brighter the sky, the darker the body
Of the stout man adjusting his wife's panorama.
Headland after headland enclosing golden tesserae
Make these bays Byzantine; halo-shaped, as if
An hour before judgement, on the last day,
When the sun proves alchemical, and the landscape
Shrivels before a goldset burning the world
And the gold reflections from the sacred letters.
Blackened joists to stables and retreats, blackened
Apses shattering in temples. Then the saints
Anonymous will stand among their removed lids;
Return to sun-warmed, stone hermitage beds,
To the temptations in gold deserts, tortures,
Tauntings before the expulsion of swart devils
And pillar-snapping in the precincts of idolaters.
Wipe off the smut, and gold will be underneath
On the last day, as the sky goes openly gold,
Earth scorches, and the olive trees grow black.

Civilised People

Camping in allocated sites, below or above archaeological sites,
designated your personal temenos, pitching the tent
within a wall so low you can step over it in flip-flops.
You get one tree for shade and your own outhouse,
complete with seatless toilet and plugless wash-basin
breeding mosquitoes glad of a meal on the doorstep.
Then you may find yourself in a sort of campsite suburbia,
with other inmates hosing down their shaded cars
along the street of pitches, just as they would
on Sunday at home while the wife starts the potatoes.
Certain campsites look as efficient as Belsen: high fences,
and ominously immaculate facilities which civilised
people will leave in the state they were conceived.
The more desolate the landscape, the more impoverished the locals,
the more lavish these holiday villages for those who
like to rough it in style; more expensive too behind their
white walls crowned with broken glass, their seasonal
surcharge and their guardians in the official T-shirt.
One hot gettone lasts two minutes in the tepid shower,
leaving you stuck, nude and soapy, several
hundred yards from your tent and another gettone.

For some people in the South, camping becomes a *modus vivendi;*
their domicile is the mobile home; an extravagant van
with a balcony to its roof, behind which they lounge
in deck-chairs during the long summer siestas.
Others hang their hammocks woven out of coloured string
in the dappled light swinging between gum trees.

Under the massive white cliff of Eraclea Minoa, they pop
their caught swordfish into a dustbin to keep cool or take
photos of their children finishing bluet-cooked rigatoni
by an open-air television hooked up to the camp electricity.
Tents with several rooms, or at least boasting a raisable
ante-chamber orange door, go up under bamboo roofs
between posts in aisles beside the sea below the gleaming cars.
Pity the poor fellow sold a pole or two short on his first trip,
forced to improvise with the guardian's rake and a clothes-line.
The campers strum guitars beside zippable arches in canvas:
they flick matches into the pine needles: they take
a communal shower in their swimming trunks and bikinis.
Under the violet blotches of the circling mirror-ball
they dance motionless with their children in the disco,
and a photographer's flash illuminates the wires
on the lighting trellis against the steep chalk face
of the cliff some ancient town has fallen off.

The Lost Garden

Her breasts are simply great
– The sort that make me grovel:
There beside her room-mate
She lies with her novel.

Is it mad of me
To envy just how intimate
Her own fingers can be
Readjusting her swimsuit?

Death is age, I reckon.
Even if I got my stomach trim,
Wouldn't I look obscene
With muscles younger than I am?

Now a slim girl stretches.
It is the chest of her man
She inadvertently touches
As he leans against the cannon.

When the rest of the gang
Leave for a club nearby,
She manages to swing
Her head to catch my eye;

But in so sweet a way
He glances back and notices
That since I'm going grey
I only merit courtesies.

Castell de Ferro

After this incredibly hot, windy spell,
When stinging sand blew in all afternoon,
It is nice to sit in the cool once more
On the airy verandah of this old hotel
Where bougainvillæa swarms towards the green
Shutters of the first-floor windows. Here,
As we finish our meal, the 'gnip-gnop'
Of ping-pong can be heard above the sigh
From the surf, since the wind has abated;
That terrible heat has lessened with its drop.
Our white-jacketed waiter takes the things away,
And a large cypress with neatly plated
Little cones releases an aroma of the night
While bent towards the awning of bamboo
Above our heads. Gently rocking below
Is the blue pool where a guest got tight
And stood with his rod, fishing there in lieu
Of the shore where the violent wind would blow
His line back in his face. But that was earlier.
Aperitifs are served to those who murmur now
At poolside tables, each beneath its parasol.
Swift lines which vanish darn the atmosphere
As martins dive for insects in the afterglow,
Though later on the bats will be more plentiful.
Behind the figtree, by the life-belt wall,
A dusty building stained with ferrous oxide
Falls into neglect; but while it rots
The pastel blocks of several very tall
Apartment buildings rise on every side,

Each balcony competing with its flower-pots.
From one of these a woman leans on a rail,
Resting slender hands on sleeves,
And between these dwellings gumtrees sway
In the gentle breeze which remains of the gale;
Beautiful trees with gaps between their leaves
Allowing limpid glimpses of the sky.

See You Later

As we drove to Broken Hill,
She spoke of the hive and its thrill
To the flower alone in the field.
The outback then revealed
An endless empty place,
But now we move at city pace
Through art-school canteens:
Damp trays and diced mixed-vegetables.

Waiting for her to get home
From balancing plates on her arm,
I turn off the set, get the bed warm,
Flip through the pages where Freda and Kurt
Combine in a number of ways.
She will be back in her white blouse
And her black skirt
Around two o'clock in the morning.
Then, by nine tomorrow,
I have to be teaching.

All day, the creators
Of posters, flyers and wanted notices
Wobble past in floppy dungarees,
While taciturn Bohemians
In overcoats which might look right on rhinos
Warn me off too intimate a crit.

I can unbutton her blouse,
Unzip the side of her skirt
As she stands in the light of the heat.
Yes, but will she be tired?
All night she is kept on her feet.

Of His Friend

What do I think of her leaning on the arm
Of somebody she likes? I can't complain.
I like her shape, I like the way her legs begin:
Lovingly the lion eats the antelope.
Don't be so tentative, I keep telling her.
Then she knows her own mind enough
To stick around and be tied down to the bed.
But it is difficult doing one job when
Your heart is set on the work you don't
Get paid for. Why do I shout and abuse her
When each and every slip-up rings a chord?
Me browsing the shops, buying too many coffees,
Shouting abuse I don't shout at myself
In case I sounded mad. The longer we're
Together, the more I associate my failings
With her presence. This has happened before.

Is it a law that love-affairs must lengthen
Into nuisances? Why do I act so critical?
Can't I resign myself to the repetition?
Won't I find some poetry in that resignation?
Still, I lift her breasts and like to do it:
It is like liking her paintings when she paints.
If only she could do nothing but. But when
She forgets whether she has left the iron on
In the house after we have driven away from it,
I could tear the leaves down from the trees.
If she's absent-minded, there's too much on
Her plate. And if her painting is tentative,
It is because she lacks the confidence
Doing nothing but might supply her with.
I do little to diminish our tensions,
Instead I make things worse, shouting Fuck it,
Fuck it when she sets fire to the toaster,
Or I preach, much as I do to my students.
Yes, it does irritate me that she mispronounces
The names of famous modern artists:
That's an Australian mannerism, a sort of
Deliberate stance. It's anti-cultural
And vaguely disapproving, to my mind,
As if it were pretentious just to have a name
That was difficult to deal with. Buladeelah
Gives her no trouble, nor any of the
Many Australian names I find unpronounceable.
How can she take so long to iron a blouse,
To wash her hair, to choose her skirt
In the morning? What do I think of her?
She can fault a poem. And I like her voice.
I like it when she slides between my legs.
At least she isn't jealous or possessive,
Or not excessively so, though slightly
On occasion, when she doesn't like the chit.
I am the same, though I won't admit it.

People Wear Their Nudity Like Clothes

1

A terracotta girl treats the restaurant
    to the sight of her loose white top.
She sits opposite her naked friend;
    a somewhat authoritarian blond
    smoking and writing postcards.
Groups of pneumatic girls pass by,
    sporting incredibly thick tussocks
    of ginger hair below their bellies.
I am busy looking under and between
    thighs and armpits
    without showing it;
    a connoisseur of
    sandy tufts and neat brushes.

Girls with sturdy breasts lean forwards
    as they dig their paddles in the water.
A head crosses the green surface.
Here comes a tummy which ends in a splash.
She enters up to her waist
    then pushes herself
    deeply into the river.
Her smooth bottom up-ends in a duck-dive,
    split by a dark slash.

2

Like the wildlife, humans disappear
    and reappear among trees,
    on the surface, along crags.
Blond children arch their backs,
    all shoulder-blades and pert arses.

Penises retract as they enter the water.
The waggling genital swings
    from a thicket of briars.
As they walk it bounces in its nest.
Here a dark line of hair
    reaches to a lean navel.
Men are divided by lines.
When men stand
    or girls bend
    there is a warm
    twinge in the mind.
How nice the breeze is
    by each pubic strand.
Naked bodies of all shapes and sizes
    queue up in the shop
    for yogurts and salamis.

3

These Neanderthal Redskin Etruscans
    from all over Europe
    break logs with rocks
    but correct proofs
    while they sunbake.
Though they sit in the steep shade,
    the rising sun inexorably
    subtracts this until they feel
    their shoulders overheat.
But Dürer was correct, and like the Etruscans
    got their long spines
    and short legs right.
Take that complex of muscles
    at the small of the back:
    even that can be lost in fat.
Still, one comes to terms
    with people's Tampax strings.

No one pretends not to look
    at the infant's hair-free vulva
    or the scar on that left nate.

4

Rose-pink, recently undressed,
    some fresh arrivals
    rub each other with a balm:
There are shadows under each breast
    and between the man's chest
    and the child on his arm.
Skinny creatures rock the dinghy.
Astraddle.
Akimbo.
Afloat.

Now some splashes turn a head
    to the white soles of swimming feet.
Foam in his crawl.
A vigorous stroke.
The artist sharpens her nude pencil.

Animal Crackers

Anchored on the stumps of mountains,
Up soars Manhattan, that glittering assemblage;
A giant barge, steel-sided,
Cleaving rivers apart, and yet,
Wherever it can, nature insinuates itself.
Weeds negotiate cracks – even Manhattan
Almost approaches wilderness at
Inwood Hill, perched on its northern tip,
Where pheasants nest, foxes prowl
On slopes once occupied by the Indians.
Off its shore there are forests and wetlands,
Including the ponds of Jamaica Bay,
Breeding baldpates, pintails,
Greater and lesser scaup, skimmers, terns,
Glossy ibises, egrets, and even visited
By the bald eagle. All the same, New Yorkers
Would not know from watching it on the box
Whether a cow was sick or not
As any hillbilly might. To the urbanite,
Farm animals are desirable, with more correspondence
Concerning them than any other perversion.
You see less of animals than people. People
Give you diseases. Animals do not sue
For alimony, nor can they get you pregnant.

Recently my mother visited New York.
She cannot see what she looks directly at,
Yet at seventy-six she managed to get
From Gramercy Park to the Bronx Zoo and back.
Having been a vet, she was more alert
To Fragonard's cow at the Met
Than handling and stuff like that.
The same was true for Dubuffet's cow at MoMA.

Seated in the sculpture garden
Next to a Maillol, off to her right
She could see a goat. Picasso's goat, I said.
Then I headed for the bookshop,
Telling her to stay put.
Back with a cut-price Muybridge,
I caught sight of her straightening up
Behind its metal rump.
Mother had goosed the goat,
Establishing when her kids would drop.
Luckily there were no guards about.

First Meditation

Black nostrils of heifers drip dark drops of blood.
Wobbly viscera land on the floor. Mr Keep
The technician lays a guinea-pig flat on its back
On a board. He hammers down the limbs
And then starts on a chicken: having nailed its wings,
He opens the stomach with one sweep of his lancet.
Crocodile scissor-tweezers lift out spleen and pancreas,
Even a beating heart. Yank, twist, snip.
He carries on methodically till everything
Lies ready for inspection: that's my mother's job.
I have been given a heart. It throbs and throbs
In my fingers. We all know about chickens
Running around in the yard without their heads.
The smell is far from pleasant – whiff of sleeping foetuses,
Offal, and a jelly used for tests.
The animals you find in a post-mortem room
Have only been put down

To find out what was wrong with them
Or to cure a herd. Beneath the microscope,
Corpuscles jostle germs. I like to watch.
People keep telling me to pull up my socks.
Dogs die in my bed and Siamese cats have fits.
In no way whatsoever can I ever be replaced
The way that pups grow into dogs and kittens into cats.
My own death will be an absolute loss to humanity,
No doubt about that. And if there's a germ going round,
There'll be no cutting me up for the benefit of the herd.

Between Functions

First he sticks his fingers down his throat,
Who in a moment must extemporise
On somebody's bath-house. His role
Is to stretch his concertina, not
To squeeze as much as Martial
Into a handful of lines. For Statius
Knows how to spout. His poems
Are articles on chi-chi villas,
Openings and events on the social
Calendar. Politically,
He is never less than correct;
Has nothing but praise for gallery
Owners, gladiators and the grandiose.
For Statius can never subtract.
How long can he spin things out?
The road of excess
Leads to the palace of Domitian.

The Watering Hole

There's a big crowd in the Beverley tonight:
Lads that sharp they look lemony
Are wearing out the crushed flower carpet.
Dappled partings and suffused crew-cuts
Here occult obsolete methods of transport.
Silhouettes removed from frosted glass
Delineate spiked fruit, flames and so forth.
The boy-scouts are about to bump the statue:
Short sleeves make biceps look the bigger,
While bike-boys look lissom in their leathers:
Boot-soles stropped against the rail.
Sheer legs are tucked beneath a chair.
Nice boys look tougher cropped of hair,
Broad girls look lovelier in their tresses.
Those with uncomfortable noses are made
Acutely aware by the knowing shake of the head
With the half-smile – 'I'm sorry, darl – .'
They make messes of the big ashtrays:
Long white filters wear their kisses.
Many of the men sport patches on their hearts
And appreciate ten-denier stay-puts,
Fuchsia blouses, camisoles and hair.
Every Sunday morning the conscientious girls
Colourise their samplers under streams of urine.
The bike-boys keep to one end of the bar,
The boy-scouts to the other – not real
Bike-boys, not genuine boy-scouts either.

Intercity

Cables lope along by streamlined carriages,
And orderly canals have shadows
Uniform with bridges. But you look out
At the backsides of places, hinder-parts
To mansions, patched together lean-tos.
Practical indecencies: underpants on tyre-stacks,
Paths to disgraces only a few people use:
The dens of clutch specialists, muffler fitters,
Barely reachable tracts of the unspeakable.
This is the unconscious side of the animal
Betrayed by things it would like to forget:
Small, scruffy woods, suitable for rape,
Deadly-looking pools, the slapdash of terraces
Which speed and distance try to sentimentalise:
Cuttings hacked through the body, dead
Lorry acreages overrun by brambles . . .

The Ballad of the Sands

She kicks off her shoes
As the season winds down.
It's cheaper on the rides,
But when she's got the blues
She usually decides
To go barefoot on the dune.

The Pelican Hotel
Boasts a good view of it
Looming over trees
Between swung swings
And children on the rungs
Of the amenities.

Trippers crack jokes,
Filling to the brim
Bins for their crisps
While balancing their smokes
On tables where the booze
Froths along its rim.

The moron on the patio
Cannot help but stare:
He leans against his minder
Afflicted with a glare
And seems to have arms
Where his legs ought to go.

To lug him or his friends
Up the steep sands,
The keeper at the gate
Loans toboggans at weekends,
Not that they accelerate
In anything but snow.

Here the sun intensifies
The tamarisk, and toe-grips
Collapse on a haunch.
The calm profile gets
Interrupted by silhouettes:
Each step setting off an avalanche.

The dune serves as prostitute
To loud sneakers now:
Hardly any foot
Of her without scuffed print.
Dogs, balls, men;
Jeans, bleached women –

They photograph toboggans
Which refuse to budge.
A dog's bark begins
To break the frail crust
Still intact, higher up
On the last ridge.

A sky swamped moon
Rises as the dune rises
Over plantations of pines.
The marram grass
Pierces her with sparse
Tufts poking up like spines.

Stiff, bleached marram,
Every plume and stalk
Shaking as the girl
Continues her solitary walk.
The bare feet fall
Without a sound.

The girl has no goal.
Savouring her wanderlust,
She brushes through the thickets
Inhabited by crickets
Till she wades the gust
Battling her skirt.

Her footprints are soon
Smoothed over by the wind
And you lose their descent
In some crater of the dune
Where the shade's crescent
Enlarges afternoon.

Boys shout bang from the ground.
But out of sight
Is clogged of sound,
And even further away
There is the sea, glittering
In stretches blurred by grey.

Flat-bottomed, bumbling
Cumuli address the coast:
Did the children pass her
At a run – tumbling
Because the steep
Impelled them all too fast?

Lower down, the dune
Gets caressed;
Losing all marks
Of upsets and mouthfuls of sand.
The breeze is the ghost of a hand
Moving over a breast.

A gnarled tree reaches
Under the skirts of a cloud
As you roam the beaches
And every tufted pass
Calling for the blue girl
Lost among the marram grass.

Orange berries glow
As the tamarisks encroach
On the dune: a slow
Drift of ripples
Volcanic in approach,
Or lava worn as a broach.

She might pick a spray
To set off her suit
As she makes her way
Through the streets to work.
Bushes of this sort
Deck the tiered court.

She wears dark tights,
And a tube skirt
Slit up the back.
Her high heels clack
Down the brick steps
By the lights.

Here the motors wait,
Easing off their brakes
And ready to accelerate
As others move across.
A sleek Rover overtakes
A double-decker bus.

Three flowered frocks
Get stranded on an island.
Someone dashes past
In a cardigan with mail
As a messenger locks
His bike to the rail.

Here the traffic
Trembles for the girl
Stepping out into it
As the lights change
And the wheels whirl
And she skips out of range.

Here the old Roman
Catches his reflection
As he glides past the bank
At the intersection
And swings round the taxi rank
In his dented Datsun.

Back in town again
After a day of triple lane,
Two direction curves,
Where the broken line
Altered sides from dip to rise
– A day full of swerves.

He drove on his own
Dazzled by the sun,
And his steering gave a groan
At each slow turn
– Groaned as in pain.
Back in town again:

A man who haunts
The venues of the young:
Lemur of his own youth,
Never mind the taunts
He may fling at himself,
On occasion staring at the truth.

Out of tune with his career,
This sham emperor
Cruises through the town
From sauna to singles bar,
Searching for some elixir
In a dented motor-car.

Pale old Roman:
He may be balding,
But he's no eagle, this one.
A hedonist at heart
With an outer shell
Which hasn't worn well.

Habitué of crowded pubs,
Connected by his eyes
To any parts in contact:
Brisk young thighs
Pushed against hips,
Reciprocating lips.

A surreptitious glance
And a half bitter smile
Establishes his stance;
A single man once more,
Answerable to no one,
What is he searching for?

The whiskey sour
In the right hotel
At the happy hour?
The attentive belle
Raised from the floor
At the end of her straw?

He is the attentive one
The lady in the navy suit
May notice drinking
At some adjacent table.
He's not that cute,
And she knows what he's thinking.

An hour later, therefore,
He seats himself gingerly
On a bench already wet
With condensation or
Some other person's sweat.
Sour steam surrounds him.

He soaks up the heat,
Tries to free his mind
Of its image of a girl
Observed on a dune
Battling the wind:
A girl like the moon.

She looked blue, beautiful.
But now his session's up.
He vacates the steam
As a blond, busty treat
In pale aertex freshens up
Each dank corner of the suite.

Here he is again,
Limper now, but clean,
Cruising through the streets
With stars in his sights
– Or are they just the lights
Reflected in his glasses?

Nice if he could score,
But he doesn't take
Enough care anyway.
The core of a pear
In his key-tray
Shouldn't be there.

Somewhere in the eighties
He lost the art of chatting up.
Getting laid is serious
For an unassuming chap
Saddled with the tastes
Of a Tiberius.

Absent-minded
When he's on the hunt,
He glides past the moon
In his Datsun saloon
With the dent at the back
And at the front.

He glides past the starred
Lugubrious hotel,
Where old turds gather
In the stair-well,
Queuing for the lecture
On the Bard.

He ought to be there,
Not heading for the disco
Along from the fair
At the far end of town,
Just up the shore
From the marram-covered dune.

The wenches go out there
In their Lycra underwear,
Soon to be upended
By the Zipper:
They shriek down chutes
And they wail on the Dipper.

The Cyclone Twist
Isn't to be missed,
But later on
They like to frisk
Around their bags
To the latest disk.

Chic teen dreams
Flicker in the beams
Of the syncopated spots
Till the fog-machine
Messes with their curls
And they join the other girls.

One of them has been
In trouble with the Law –
Not for nothin serious, mind.
Call one a whore,
But the rest are amateurs,
Partially inclined.

And though she would rather
Be sampling the rides,
The one in the turquoise
Hiccups and confides
In the eager gentleman
Who could be her father.

She spits as she chatters,
Passionate and squiffy;
Pressing where it matters
And giving him a sniffy;
Boasting that she lifted
Her perfume from Boots.

Wonderful sensation
Of spittle on his cheek
Spat from such lips,
And he likes the reek
Of tobacco on her breath
As she slags off probation.

She hasn't done time,
And she's not on the game,
And she has a feller,
But they're all the same
– Young men at least:
They get you all creased.

With an older bloke though
A girl can depend
On a drink for herself
And one for her friend:
What matters at the disco
Is what you've got to spend.

You seat her in the dark
Of your comfortable saloon,
Slap in a cassette,
Turn the volume down
And take her to the car-park
Out by the dune.

Uncertain what she'll ask,
You offer her a swig
From your flask;
And then in lieu
Of further talk
You suggest a walk.

The big full moon
Diminishes the stars,
Hones every shadow
To a knife's edge.
A tree's dead spars
Appear dim though.

What is it moves
Out of the sand
In which it has sunk?
It's only a trunk.
Utter darkness
Rustles in the groves.

The moon shines bright
Between grey fleeces:
Her radiance increases
The bowl of the dune,
Felt as very large
Even in the light.

She slows down the cloud,
Blazes on the creatures
Sunk in their gloom.
Imperiously proud,
She travels by the light
Of her features.

Having spilt love,
You're too dazed to move;
And though you should be brisk
The moon numbs your feet,
Roots you to the spot
By the tamarisk:

The place off the track
Where she said
She'd had enough
And wanted to go back;
The place where you dug
The shallow trough.

She may not follow,
But you must get away
From the hollow
Where she started to shout.
Time is the sand,
And yours is running out.

Nothing shines so brightly
As the white ball of light
Bearing down from afar.
Prints remain visible
On this illuminated night.
You must get back to the car.

Melancholy hooting
Floats across the motionless
Ripples which cover
The flanks of the dune
You stumble over.
Dawn will come soon.

Next will come the minder
Who tugs the moron
Through the sandy places
In a hired toboggan,
With little else to do
But follow up your traces.

You are completely alone
With the dune and the moon:
Sufficiently high
To catch the lighthouse
Many miles away
Flashing once, then twice.

On this saddleback of sand
Gusts and eddies move
Her grains into a collar-bone;
A long, curved ridge
With a sharp edge above
The steep plunge down.

The pine plantations sough.
You are about to go down
Into a cleavage of time
Occluded by a cloud
Fashioned like a clown
Which is changing even now.

It has become the skull
Of some tormented girl,
Her mouth open wide.
The moon disturbs her mane,
Passes through the fringes
Of her brain.

She gets lost inside,
And the world goes dark
Before you get back
Through the pines
To the carpark.
Everything looks black.

But she sails through the cloud,
And her radiance comes back;
And the whole dune glints
And shimmers as you'd wish it,
If those damn prints
Didn't somehow blemish it.

Creakings in the pine trees.
You slip past the corpses
Of wart-hogs –
Or are they logs?
You just make the Datsun
But can't find the keys.

You can't have locked them in!
Not in the ignition!
Absent bloody minded
By your own admission,
Now you're stuck, blinded
By their dangling.

For in between the blackouts
Perpetrated by the clouds,
As a chill enshrouds
The car-park in silence,
The moon grows intense
And uses these to dazzle you.